CW01082838

Original title:

Walk a Little Slower


Copyright © 2024 Book Fairy Publishing

Editor: Theodor Taimla

Author: Sandra Squirrel

ISBN HARDBACK: 978-9916-759-58-5

ISBN PAPERBACK: 978-9916-759-59-2

## Laid-back Routes

Winding paths and rolling hills,
Where time lazily spills.
Sunset whispers in the breeze,
Painting gold on autumn trees.

Meandering rivers softly glide,
Inviting dreams to coincide.
Nature's ease and tranquil tunes,
Dancing under silver moons.

## Navigating Stillness

Silence speaks in restful tones,
Softly echoing through stones.
Moonlight drapes the quiet earth,
Weighing hearts with gentle worth.

Echoes of a distant night,
Grounded by the stars' soft light.
Navigating voids serene,
Where whispered hopes reweave the scene.

## Steps in Retrospect

Footprints trace a path behind,
Memories in shadows find.
Lessons learned in twilight's glow,
To the past, our thoughts bestow.

Journeys marked by fleeting sands,
Held within our gentle hands.
Stories etched in silent ground,
In those steps, the moments found.

## Gentle Pilgrimage

Travelers on a silent quest,
Seeking peace, a soul at rest.
Mountains watch our pensive pace,
Silent guardians of our space.

Every step a prayer unheard,
Each breath merging with the word.
Gentle winds and thoughtful skies,
Guard the pilgrim's quiescent cries.

# Steps of Serenity

In gardens where the lilies glow,
Under stars that softly show,
Steps of calm through night's embrace,
Find serenity in this space.

Whispers of the evening air,
Gentle, tender, without care,
Walking slow beneath the skies,
Peace reflected in your eyes.

Tender moments in the dusk,
Feelings pure, free from husk,
Serenity in every tread,
With dreams we softly spread.

# Pathways in Time

Through the ages we have roamed,
On pathways carved and seldom known,
Echoes linger from the past,
Memories that ever last.

With each step, the stories merge,
Times collide, and tides emerge,
Footprints of the years gone by,
Tracing paths beneath the sky.

Moments whisper, ages blend,
Journeys start, and journeys end,
Timeless rivers intertwine,
Pathways through the sands of time.

# Gentle Footprints

On the sands of dawn's first light,
Gentle footprints come in sight,
Softly etched by morning's glow,
Tales untold from long ago.

Quiet steps through fields of green,
Whispers of what might have been,
Every mark a silent trace,
In the earth, a fleeting grace.

Paths entwined with hope and dreams,
Through the meadows, past the streams,
Gentle footprints lead the way,
To the promise of the day.

## Meandering Moments

In a world where rivers wind,
Meandering moments we will find,
Silent streams of thought and flow,
Lives entwined where waters go.

Drifting through a sunlit glen,
Moments pause and start again,
Every bend a new surprise,
Echoes dance beneath the skies.

Through the valleys, over hills,
Time meanders, softly fills,
Lives with fleeting, precious gems,
Meandering as daylight dims.

## Harmonious Hikes

In forests deep, the whispers flow,
With each step, the wonders grow.
Beneath the canopy, life thrives,
Nature's rhythm, our hearts revive.

Mountains loom with majesty,
Rivers hum their sweet decree.
Echoes of the wildlife call,
Harmony in nature's hall.

Leaves in symphony softly play,
Guiding us along the way.
Breathing in the purest air,
Harmonious hikes, beyond compare.

## Sinslow Strolls

In the evening's gentle glow,
Shadows dance, and time moves slow.
Cobblestones beneath our feet,
Sinslow lanes, where lovers meet.

Lanterns cast a soft embrace,
Illuminating every face.
Windows whisper tales old,
Strolling through the stories told.

Pause to hear the river's song,
Guiding us as we belong.
Hand in hand through twilight's scene,
Sinslow strolls, a dream serene.

## Mindful Movements

With each breath, a moment true,
Mindful movements, skies so blue.
Steps aligned with heart and soul,
Peaceful paths we shall unroll.

Silent woods and tranquil streams,
Flowing through our midnight dreams.
Nature's whispers, gentle calls,
Mindful in these ancient halls.

Balance found in every stride,
Harmony we seek inside.
In the stillness, wisdom gleams,
Mindful movements, life's pure beams.

## Traversing Tranquility

Down the path where flowers bloom,
Whispers in the gentle gloom.
Tranquil steps through meadows wide,
Peaceful worlds we can't divide.

Birdsong lifts our spirits high,
Arching rainbows in the sky.
Streams that murmur tales old,
Traversing realms of quiet gold.

Every bend a new embrace,
Calmness found in nature's grace.
Journeys in this silent spree,
Traversing tranquil reverie.

# The Calm Trek

In twilight's gentle breeze, we stray,
Guided by soft whispers, not dismay.
Stars illuminate our winding path,
Drawing silhouettes in night's rough draft.

Mountains peak through veils of mist,
Each step a promise, a silent tryst.
Oceans whisper secrets in the wind,
Nature's song begins where colors blend.

Through forests dense and calm, we glide,
Companions to the moon, our gentle guide.
Rivers hum their dull refrain,
Echoes of the earth's vast domain.

# Footfall Echoes

Beneath the ancient canopy, paths unwind,
Footfalls echo, leave worries behind.
Whispers of the leaves, a soothing sound,
Nature's melodies all around.

Granite boulders cast shadows long,
Each step, a verse in nature's song.
Streams murmur secrets, ages old,
Stories in their waters, pure and cold.

The forest breathes with ancient lore,
Every step reveals more and more.
Mysteries dance in morning mist,
Nature's beauty, we can't resist.

# Steady Swirls

Swirling leaves in autumn's grace,
A dance eternal, nature's embrace.
Golden hues and coppered light,
A tapestry woven, pure delight.

Winds hum through branches, tall and grand,
Nature's art in every land.
Leaves descend in gentle whirl,
A timeless dance, an endless twirl.

Through meadows vast and rivers wide,
Swirls paint the landscape, far and nigh.
In each curve, a story lies,
Whispered softly as the day dies.

## Mellow Trails

Through sunlit meadows, paths we weave,
In mellow trails, time grants reprieve.
Each step a bond with earth so old,
In tranquil moments, hearts unfold.

Gentle hills and valleys deep,
Secrets in the flora, keep.
Harmony in quiet tones,
Nature's presence, known in stones.

Morning dew and evening charms,
A soothing journey, free from harms.
In the stillness, wisdom grows,
On mellow trails, life's rhythm flows.

## Soft Ventures

In the hush of twilight's kiss,
Whispers dance in gentle breeze.
Dreams alight on wings of bliss,
Hearts find calm, where moments seize.

Boundless skies, serene and vast,
Hope takes flight, where shadows part.
In the stillness, love's forecast,
Guides us through, both near and far.

Tender steps on paths unknown,
Softly tread through meadows fair.
Every seed of kindness sown,
Blooms to life in twilight's glare.

# Serene Travels

Morning dew on petals bright,
Paths unfold in sunlight's glow.
Nature's call to hearts' delight,
Journeys start where rivers flow.

Footsteps brushed by fragrant lands,
Echoes of the ancient song.
Silent whispers, fate's commands,
Guide our souls where we belong.

Majestic peaks and valleys green,
Glistening under heavens blue.
Eyes that see the unseen scene,
Find tranquility anew.

## Pondered Paths

Wandering through the woods of thought,
In the quiet, wisdom speaks.
Lessons in each moment caught,
Wisdom found in ancient creaks.

Questions linger on the breeze,
Paths unknown, yet trod before.
Every step, with patient ease,
Leads to answers found once more.

Mysteries in every leaf,
Stories written on the bark.
Journeys through both joy and grief,
Light the way, even when dark.

## Embracing the Journey

Through valleys deep and mountains high,
Life's vast canvas we explore.
Every heartbeat, every sigh,
Prints adventures evermore.

Embrace the turns, both sharp and kind,
For in each twist, the spirit grows.
In the search, much more we find,
Than simple paths or gentle flows.

Hand in hand with time we stride,
Learning, loving, as we go.
Trust the compass deep inside,
Guides to places we should know.

## Stately Strides

In woodlands deep, the giants rise,
Their branches trace the twilight skies.
Beneath their shade, where roots entwine,
The silent steps of passing time.

Ancient trees in whispered groves,
Guard secrets that the river knows.
Leaves that flutter, tales they weave,
Of journeys that the years conceive.

Through the meadows, stately strides,
Glimpses of dawn where beauty hides.
Tranquil breaths and golden rays,
Moments etched in endless days.

## Charmed Chases

Sunlight dances on the fields,
A playful chase that morning yields.
Charmed by laughter, winds arise,
Tickling clouds in sapphire skies.

Enchanted by the echoes clear,
Nature's symphony draws near.
Whispers soft through rustling leaves,
Magic lingers, hearts believe.

Mystic paths where dreams align,
Following the stars' design.
Hand in hand, through dusk's embrace,
Lost in timeless, charmed chase.

## Soft Stepping Stones

In streams that murmur lullabies,
Soft stepping stones in moonlit guise.
Guiding feet through liquid dreams,
Where twilight's gentle essence gleams.

Pebbles glow beneath the night,
Pathways forged in silver light.
Echoes of a river's song,
Leading wanderers along.

Each smooth stone, a keeper's key,
Unlocking realms of mystery.
Softly treading, whispers known,
Across the quiet stepping stones.

# Linger with Breath

In morning's hush, the world awakes,
Breath serene the dawn remakes.
Veils of mist on silent lakes,
Nature's hand a picture takes.

Moments held in gentle sighs,
Ephemeral as the breeze flies.
In the stillness, hearts align,
Temporary, yet divine.

Lingering breaths a soft caress,
Inhale love, exhale stress.
Through life's dance, we interweave,
Eternity in breaths we leave.

### Soothing Trails

Underneath the verdant shade,
Where whispering winds have played.
Steps so gentle, quiet, kind,
Leave the world's coarse noise behind.

Streams that gurgle, songs so clear,
Lavender blooms drawing near.
Soft as feather, paths unwind,
Peace in every step we find.

Golden rays through branches peek,
Nourishing the souls we seek.
Find a solace, pockets deep,
Lulling trails to restful sleep.

# Harmonious Paths in Motion

Hands held close through silent wood,
Rhythms found, as hearts breathe good.
In the breeze, our spirits glide,
Nature's song, our only guide.

Leaves crunch softly, melodies pure,
Wonders whisper to allure.
Through the dance where pines converge,
Life and love in every urge.

Twilight dips in hues aglow,
Harmonious paths, to and fro.
Every step, a lullaby,
Bound by earth, beneath the sky.

# Steps in Time

Traceries of ancient lines,
Echoes loud through towering pines.
With each step a tale we weave,
In the lore of time, we cleave.

Phantom shadows, markers old,
Secrets on the paths unfold.
Steps in time, we gently trace,
Every moment, every place.

Cobbled stones and worn-out trails,
Mossy paths where wisdom hails.
In the pulse of fleeting rhymes,
Lives are lived in steps through time.

### Whispers of the Trail

Soft the whisper, trails align,
Guiding souls where dreams rewind.
Every turn a tale to hear,
Whispers cloaked in nature's cheer.

Dappled light on gold and green,
Paths unfold, both heard and seen.
Sighs of ages, secrets frail,
Upon a whisper, stories sail.

Hearts attuned, in step we go,
Silent voices, gentle flow.
On the wind, the myths prevail,
Life is sung on every trail.

## Slow Dance of Life

In the hush of twilight's glow,
Leaves rustle a gentle song.
Steps are measured, hearts beat slow,
As time around us lingers long.

A waltz of whispers fills the air,
Soft moments hold us tight.
We're entwined in evening's care,
Beneath the tender light.

Pausing here, we breathe it in,
The rhythm of the night.
Letting go where dreams begin,
To dance till morning's light.

# Byway Dreams

On winding paths where stories blend,
Steps trace a quiet line.
Through fields where the roadward bends,
Our restless hearts align.

In shadows cast by wander's grace,
The moonlight gently beams.
Echoes of this transient place,
Weave our woven dreams.

Under stars that softly wink,
We tread with hopeful gleams.
Beyond horizons, on the brink,
Of endless byway dreams.

## A Softened Pace

Where silence meets the whispering trees,
Soft steps of time unfold.
Moments shared in gentle breeze,
A quiet tale retold.

Beneath a sky of changing hues,
Life's rhythm finds its place.
In tranquil waves of dusk's embrace,
We savor a softened pace.

Through shadows long and light's retreat,
The world spins slow and sure.
In every heartbeat, every street,
Our journey finds its cure.

# Easing Through Canopies

Beneath the arch of verdant dreams,
Light filters through the leaves.
Each whispering breeze a story weaves,
Of nights the forest keeps.

A dance of shadows, soft and kind,
Plays out upon the ground.
In gentle steps, we're intertwined,
By nature's soothing sound.

Through forest's heart, we find our way,
In whispers, time agrees.
A journey marked by light and shade,
Easing through the canopies.

# Gentle Stroll Through Time

Through epochs old and tales untold,
We wander paths where dreams unfold.
In whispers soft, the decades blend,
A gentle touch from time, a friend.

Each step we take, the years unwind,
Memories in cobwebbed corners find.
A tapestry of moments spun,
With every sunrise, time's begun.

The clocks may tick, the hours flow,
But in our hearts, true moments grow.
An ancient song sings through the eons,
Preserving echoes, time's own cons.

With every breath, the past revives,
In nature's rhythms, life's archive.
No rush, no race, just moments fine,
A gentle stroll through threads of time.

## Pensive Footsteps

On cobblestone paths, where thoughts unwind,
A journey traced in tender kind.
Each step, a question, softly posed,
In twilight hues, the heart exposed.

With every stride, the mind explores,
Through memory's halls, forgotten doors.
A silent journey, deep delight,
Footsteps echo in the night.

In quiet moments, shadows meld,
With pensive thoughts, our souls are held.
A dance of mind and spirit bright,
In moonlit realms, our truths take flight.

As dawn approaches, whispers fade,
But still, the peace in footsteps laid.
A tranquil path, where heartbeats blend,
In pensive strides, our souls transcend.

# Reflective Routes

The road ahead, a mirrored view,
Where past and present merge in hue.
Life's winding routes, reflections sewn,
In every step, the seeds are sown.

A path illuminated by our dreams,
Beneath the stars, where vision gleams.
Each turn reveals a hidden truth,
A guiding light from tender youth.

With every mile, reflections grow,
On roads unknown, where breezes blow.
A journey traced in hearts and minds,
In mirrored shadows, solace finds.

The echoes of our steps remain,
In whispered winds, a sweet refrain.
Reflective routes, where futures blend,
In every journey, find your friend.

# Calm Coppice

Beneath the arch of verdant green,
A tranquil grove, a hidden scene.
Soft whispers in the leaves ignite,
A calm within, a soft respite.

Amidst the rustling, gentle breeze,
A fellowship of silent trees.
In nature's arms, our spirits rest,
In calm coppice, we are blessed.

The forest hums a lulling tune,
As shadows play beneath the moon.
A quietude in bark embraced,
Serenity in wood's soft lace.

Among the roots, where life does spring,
A harmony with earth's own ring.
In this stillness, find your peace,
In calm coppice, worries cease.

# The Art of the Saunter

In the dawn's early light,
We wander, hearts aglow,
Down trails where dreams take flight,
And gentle breezes blow.

With steps both slow and sure,
We cherish every sound,
In this space, unblurred, pure,
Where peace and joy are found.

Leaves whisper ancient tales,
Of ages past and gone,
And in their soft exhales,
We find the strength to dawn.

No rush, no race to win,
Just moments blessed, serene,
In nature's gentle din,
Our souls are washed, pristine.

This art of walking slow,
By forest, stream, and glen,
A treasure few may know,
Yet craved by hearts of men.

# Timeless Treads

Shoes worn by passage time,
Each mark a story's touch,
Across landscapes and climes,
In steps that mean so much.

Pathways old yet renewed,
With every gentle stride,
Memories interlude,
With whispers as our guide.

Stones weathered by the years,
Echo our fleeting pace,
In midst of joy and tears,
We find a sacred space.

Through forests lush and green,
And deserts vast and dry,
Our timeless treads are seen,
Beneath the open sky.

Journey not for the fast,
But for the patient soul,
Embrace each moment's cast,
To make the wander whole.

# Gentle Pathways

A pathway soft and kind,
Unfolds at forest's edge,
Invites the wandering mind,
To silence solemn pledge.

Where footsteps tread with grace,
And nature whispers low,
Sunlight in dappled lace,
Through leaves that gently flow.

Each turn and bend reveal,
A slowly waking world,
Where all our hearts conceal,
In layers calm, unfurled.

Birdsong and leafy sighs,
Accompany our way,
As day turns to goodbyes,
And dusk begins to play.

In these sweet paths we find,
A refuge, soft embrace,
For weary heart and mind,
In nature's quiet space.

## Unrushed Destinations

In places far yet near,
Where time itself stands still,
We travel without fear,
And savor every thrill.

Mountains rise, grand and tall,
Valleys spread lush and wide,
In each we hear the call,
Of journeys side by side.

No haste in reaching there,
Nor urgency in speed,
Just moments rich and rare,
In every thought and deed.

Through meadows, rivers wide,
And skies of endless blue,
Our hearts and worlds collide,
In steps both pure and true.

Unrushed we find the way,
To destinations deep,
Where souls can safely stay,
And dreams in silence keep.

## Pacing Through Peace

Quiet pathways woven through the trees,
Whispers of the wind carry gentle pleas.
Feet find rhythm, a harmony so sweet,
in the tranquil dance of heartbeats.

Softness cradles every stride we take,
as morning sun begins to wake.
Leaves flutter down like dreams on breeze,
Pacing through peace, we move with ease.

Gentle shadows merge with light,
In this place, all feels just right.
Time moves slowly, breath by breath,
Leading us towards a calm caress.

## Moments on the Move

Each step a tale of fleeting grace,
In moments on the move, we trace.
Life unfolds in waves and curves,
As we dance through time's reserves.

Paths of wonder, endless skies,
Look below and see how time flies.
Transient glances, the world's grand stage,
In corridors of unknown age.

Every move a fleeting frame,
Captured in a whispering name.
Journeys weave the fabric fine,
Life in motion, pure design.

# The Ease of Steps

In the ease of steps, we wander free,
Through endless fields where dreams can be.
The earth beneath, a faithful guide,
As we traverse the countryside.

Whispered winds and gentle sun,
Walk with us 'til day is done.
No burden heavy, no fear to test,
Here in steps, we find our rest.

Silence sings its mellow tune,
Underneath a watchful moon.
Every stride, so soft and clear,
Lullabies that draw us near.

## Harmony in Each Footfall

Harmony in each footfall blends,
With nature's chorus, it extends.
Mountains high and valleys low,
Every step a sacred flow.

Birds above and streams below,
In every move, their songs bestow.
Find your pace and close your eyes,
Feel the bond under skies.

Symphony of earthly tones,
Every stride—the world's own.
Graceful walks in tune with all,
Harmony in every little call.

## Creeping Contemplations

In shadows deep, the thoughts arise,
Silken threads through darkened skies.
Silent whispers fill the night,
Secrets murmur out of sight.

Moonlight dances, soft and pale,
On paths where spirits often trail.
In corners dark, reflections hide,
Where contemplation does abide.

Voices carried by the breeze,
Soft as rustling autumn leaves.
Ebbing fears and flowing dreams,
In the stillness, wisdom gleams.

Figures pass in twilight hues,
Where time bends and old renews.
Echoes lost in space and time,
Creeping thoughts in quiet rhyme.

Veil of silence draws around,
Hushed the world, without a sound.
In the depths of night, hearts ponder,
Creeping contemplations wander.

## Ease of Existence

With dawn's embrace, a tranquil start,
Nature whispers to the heart.
Birdsong weaves through morning light,
Gently breaking through the night.

Ripples play on water's face,
Mirroring a calm embrace.
Breath of life in every breeze,
Melodies bring gentle ease.

Sunlit meadows, rolling green,
Laughter where the light is seen.
Moments pause, and time delays,
In the ease of golden days.

Shadows stretch as daylight fades,
Casting soft and soothing shades.
Harmony in dusk's sweet kiss,
Existence wrapped in simple bliss.

Stars emerge in twilight's fold,
Stories in the night retold.
Life's pure rhythm, gentle sway,
Ease of existence, night and day.

# Lingering Lanes

Wandering down old cobblestone,
A silent path, I'm not alone.
Memories pressed in every crack,
Whispers from a distant track.

Tall trees lining either side,
Guardians of the space they hide.
Leaves that dance in sunlight's gleam,
Tales that linger in a dream.

Footfalls echo soft and true,
With every step, a world renews.
Ancient voices, soft and clear,
Speak of joys and shed a tear.

Under arches ivy-clad,
Shadows from the past are glad.
Every corner, every twist,
Moments lost and moments missed.

As the sky turns hues of gold,
Stories on these lanes unfold.
Lingering here, hearts are free,
In these lanes, our history.

## Soulful Saunters

Underneath the twilight's veil,
Where the world begins to pale,
Steps align with nature's voice,
Every heartbeat, every choice.

Paths that wind through silver streams,
Dancing softly in moonbeams.
Souls entwined with whispering leaves,
Where the heart a song receives.

Stars imbue the night with grace,
Lighting up each sacred place.
Peace in every step we take,
In the soulful saunters we make.

Whispers in the evening air,
Echoes of a silent prayer.
Feet find rhythm, pure and slow,
To the night, our spirits flow.

Journey through the endless night,
Guided by the softest light.
In these saunters, hearts align,
Soul and stars forever shine.

# Calmly Ahead

With morning's gentle, quiet grace,
The day begins, a tranquil place.
Soft whispers in the dawn's soft light,
Lead calmly through the fading night.

A path unfolds, serene and clear,
Guided by a calm frontier.
Each step, a quiet, measured beat,
In harmony, hearts gently meet.

The sun ascends with tender glow,
As moments merge, and spirits flow.
In calm pursuit, the day ahead,
Awakes, in peace, where dreams are led.

No rush, no haste, just steady stride,
In life's vast sea, we're gently tied.
With every breath, a calm embrace,
We journey forth in perfect grace.

## Tranquil Treads


Amidst the whispering of trees,
In nature's haven, at perfect ease.
Our footsteps soft on mossy bed,
With tranquil treads where dreams are led.

The river's song a soothing hum,
A gentle rhythm, a natural drum.
We wander where the wild things grow,
In peace, our hearts and spirits flow.

Each leaf that falls, a silent prayer,
In moments still, we're wholly there.
Through forest deep and sunlit glades,
We walk in peace, where time abates.

With every step, tranquility,
Unfolds its tender mystery.
Our souls aligned with earth's soft thread,
We journey forth, where love is fed.

# Leisurely Trails

Through fields of green and skies so wide,
On leisurely trails, we gently glide.
A timeless pace, a gentle flow,
With every step, the world we know.

The sun above, a guiding light,
As day unfolds from morning bright.
In harmony, we find our way,
On trails where peace and love convey.

The path ahead, both new and old,
With stories vivid, yet untold.
In stillness, we embrace the now,
On leisurely trails, we softly vow.

To wander free, with hearts so light,
In day and dusk, from morn to night.
In steps unmeasured, slow and true,
We find our bliss in skies so blue.

# Sauntering Paths

With gentle step, we slowly wend,
On sauntering paths, where journeys blend.
Through meadows bright and forests deep,
In wandering thoughts, our spirits keep.

The world in hues of green and gold,
The sky a canvas, vast, untold.
In silence, nature sings its song,
On sauntering paths, we drift along.

Each bend, a promise of the new,
In whispered winds, our dreams renew.
With every turn and gentle stride,
We dance with life, our hearts our guide.

No need for haste, no rush, no race,
In every step, we find our place.
On sauntering paths, where moments blend,
In peace and love, our souls transcend.

# Idyllical Paths

Underneath the emerald trees,
Soft whispers in the gentle breeze,
Nature sings in sweet repose,
Where the tranquil river flows.

Golden hues at daylight's brink,
Majestic moments on the sink,
Pastel skies at dawn so wide,
A serene and blissful ride.

Crimson leaves in autumn's clutch,
Vivid colors softly touch,
Footsteps on the earthen trail,
Idyllic paths in calm detail.

Wildflowers in summer's dance,
Meadows hold a quiet trance,
Echoes from the verdant glen,
Peace restored to hearts again.

Stars bloom in the twilight's keep,
Dreams unfold while nature's sleep,
Idyllic paths, a gentle call,
Heaven's gift, bestowed on all.

## Schritte der Ruhe

In des Abends sachte Stille,
Ruht die Welt, in sanftem Wille,
Leise Schritte durch die Zeit,
Finden in der Ruhe Freud.

Beruhigt glänzt der Sterne Flut,
Nächtliches Licht in stiller Glut,
Durch die Wälder sanft gelenkt,
Zeit vergessen, tief versenkt.

Im Schattenreich der Bäume stehn,
Sich die Geister still umwehn,
Und im Herzensgrund erwacht,
Freiheit in der Dunkelheit.

Mondschein malt ein stilles Licht,
Durch die Stille, wo man spricht,
Ohne Worte, Nur Gefühl,
Schritte der Ruhe, sanftes Spiel.

In der Dämmerung verweilen,
Einzeln' Schritte, Zeit sich teilen,
In des Friedens sanftem Reich,
Fliehen Sorgen, sacht und gleich.

# Rambling Reverie

Distant hills with lavender sheen,
Mists that cloak the valley green,
Wandering hearts in silent plea,
Lost within their reverie.

Songs of sparrows fill the morn,
Nature's symphony is born,
Dappled rays through canopies,
Whispers of the ancient trees.

Rolling fields, a golden sprawl,
Endless dreams in nature's call,
Drifting minds find solace here,
In the pathways, ever near.

Breezes carry tales untold,
Melancholy intertwined with gold,
Rest beneath the azure sky,
As the thoughts like clouds drift by.

Evening falls, a gentle sigh,
Stars ignite the velvet sky,
Rambling through these reveries,
Our souls find tranquil harmonies.

# Poised Voyages

On the edge of twilight's shore,
Ready hearts seek to explore,
Unknown lands and boundless seas,
Poised for voyages like these.

Sailing through the winds of change,
Endless dreams within our range,
Horizons blend in colors vast,
Journeys of the mind contrast.

Mountains tall and rivers wide,
Ventures take us on a ride,
Bound by hope and courage bright,
Voyages feed the soul's light.

Mystic paths through time and space,
Every step, a new embrace,
Charting courses through the night,
Symbols in the stars' delight.

Come the dawn, the voyage ends,
Trailing thoughts and newfound friends,
Poised for more, our spirits free,
Voyages to eternity.

# Deliberate Wanders

In shadows long, the path unfolds,
Where secrets dance, and tales untold.
With steps so light, the heart explores,
Through ancient woods, to distant shores.

Leaves whisper low, the wind's embrace,
In these deep woods, we find our place.
Stars above, with guiding lights,
We weave our dreams in velvet nights.

Hearts aligned with nature's pace,
In every step, a world we trace.
Conscious moves beneath the skies,
We breathe in wonder, deeply sighs.

Through mist and moon, our quest remains,
In quiet walks, we break our chains.
Journey's end, a mystery bright,
In love and dreams, we find our light.

With eyes that see beyond the veils,
We roam through whispers, ancient trails.
In silent shares, the truth it finds,
In deliberate wanders, free our minds.

# Footsteps Through Silence

In the hush of dawn's first light,
We trace our steps, embracing night.
Through fields of dew, and morning's grace,
We walk in silence, find our place.

Footsteps soft on pathways clear,
In stillness, we confront our fear.
The world in pause, a sacred sound,
In silence deep, our souls are found.

Beneath the sky, so vast and true,
Our hearts align with hidden view.
In quiet ways, the truth reveals,
Footsteps through silence gently heals.

Mountains high and valleys low,
In every step, our spirits grow.
To listen deep, the world within,
Footsteps through silence, life begins.

Through echoing halls of timeless space,
In every step, a soft embrace.
With courage found in silent might,
We tread unseen paths of light.

# Unrushed Horizons

Horizons stretch in colors grand,
Unrushed and free, we take our stand.
The morning sun, its gentle rise,
Our journey starts beneath blue skies.

With measured steps, we onward go,
Through verdant fields and rivers flow.
In every pause, a world reveals,
In unrushed moments, time it heals.

The sea in calm and mountains proud,
A symphony without a crowd.
In nature's arms, we dream and rest,
Unhurried hearts, we find we're blessed.

In twilight hues, the day's embrace,
We trace the stars, we find our place.
In every breath, the calm we find,
Unrushed horizons, peace of mind.

With gentle eyes and open hearts,
We weave our dreams in nature's art.
In stillness deep, the truth within,
Unrushed horizons, life begins.

## Dreams on the Ground

In fields where wildflowers bloom so bright,
We plant our dreams in morning light.
With hands and hearts, we sow the seeds,
Dreams on the ground, our humble needs.

Beneath the sky, both vast and grand,
We cultivate with gentle hand.
In every sprout, a hope anew,
Dreams on the ground, the earth we knew.

Raindrops kiss, the soil they embrace,
In nature's arms, we find our place.
Roots dig deep, in sacred bond,
Dreams on the ground, a world beyond.

With patience pure, we watch them grow,
In time, our dreams begin to show.
In every leaf, in every sound,
Dreams on the ground, the truth is found.

The sun descends, yet dreams remain,
In whispers soft, through earth and rain.
With every dawn, a promise crowned,
Dreams on the ground, in love profound.

# Pace With Grace

In every step, a measured beat,
Through winding paths of earthen treat,
We walk with time, in quiet space,
And learn to move with gentle grace.

The rush of life, we set aside,
Embrace the stillness, let it guide,
With open hearts and steady mind,
We find the peace, for which we pined.

Through forests deep and hills so high,
Beneath the vast and hopeful sky,
Each moment whispers, take your ease,
In nature's lap, our souls appease.

With every breath, a calm renews,
The hurried pace, we long eschew,
In harmony with life's own song,
Forever present, where we belong.

So tread the earth with mindful care,
And let your spirit roam laid bare,
For in the dance of life's embrace,
We find our joy, and pace with grace.

## Murmurs in the Meadow

In fields where wildflowers bloom bright,
The whispers echo through the light,
Soft murmurs in the meadow's sigh,
A gentle song beneath the sky.

The breeze, it carries tales untold,
Of mornings fresh, and evenings gold,
Each blade of grass, a quiet rhyme,
Unfolding stories, lost in time.

With every step, the earth rebounds,
A symphony of subtle sounds,
Where creatures small, in shadows play,
And nature's secrets softly sway.

An orchestra of life is spun,
Beneath the face of warming sun,
The brook that babbles near and far,
Joins in the murmurs where we are.

So linger in the meadow sweet,
Let nature's hum your senses greet,
For in this realm of verdant glow,
The soul's true peace begins to grow.

# Journeys Unhurried

The path ahead, a winding way,
Where moments pause and gently stay,
No rush is there to reach the end,
For each small step, our hearts commend.

Beneath the sky, so wide and clear,
We walk through life without a fear,
Embracing detours, sights unseen,
In every turn, a gift serene.

With patience worn like sacred thread,
The stories of our lives are spread,
In harmonies both sweet and kind,
We etch our tales for all to find.

The journey slow, yet full of grace,
We meet each curve with soft embrace,
And in the stillness, we discern,
The endless lessons we can learn.

So let us wander, unrestrained,
Through realms where beauty is unfeigned,
For in these journeys unhurried,
Our spirits find what's most desired.

# Dances with Patience

In quiet steps, we find our beat,
A dance with patience, calm and sweet,
Where every sway and gentle bend,
In time becomes a loyal friend.

No need to rush, the rhythm's kind,
With every turn, our hearts align,
To melodies that softly play,
And guide us through each tranquil day.

The world may hurry, spin around,
But in this dance, we're firmly bound,
To moments pure and softly spun,
That bless each breath, till day is done.

In every gesture, slow and true,
We touch the sky, embrace the blue,
A waltz that stretches through our lives,
And in its grace, true peace derives.

So take my hand, let's gently move,
In dances with the patience grove,
For in this rhythm, hearts will find,
A lasting love, both sweet and kind.

## Wander at Ease

Beneath the sky with stars alight,
We roam with hearts unburdened, free.
The path is soft, the air is light,
Our souls are like the open sea.

We drift among the whispering trees,
Their leaves a song of gentle breeze.
Time loses hold as we find peace,
Wanderers in moments, at ease.

Each step a dance, no rush, no race,
In nature's arms, a warm embrace.
A journey shared, yet solely ours,
Counting minutes, counting stars.

The moon above, a guide so bright,
Illuminates our silent flight.
No map we need, no compass drawn,
Just trust in night, and coming dawn.

In twilight's glow, we feel alive,
Embracing all that walks beside.
With every breath, we sense release,
To wander far, to wander at ease.

## Graceful Strides

Upon the path where shadows play,
The sunlight kisses feet so light.
We move with grace, as night meets day,
Our steps a whisper, soft and bright.

Each stride we take, a dancer's leap,
Across the fields where flowers peep.
Their colors blend with evening skies,
In graceful strides, our spirits rise.

With gentle poise and quiet charm,
We roam the world, a dance disarmed.
No need for haste, no rush, no train,
For in each step, there's joy, not strain.

We glide where rivers meet the shore,
And listen to their timeless roar.
Their tales of yore, in currents wide,
Reflect our paths, our graceful stride.

The journey's end we do not seek,
In every step, life's moments speak.
With measured moves through time we ride,
Forever bound in graceful stride.

## Strolling Through Ages

On ancient roads where shadows fall,
We walk with echoes of the past.
Each footfall soft, each memory calls,
Through endless time our steps are cast.

The stones we tread, tales silently tell,
Of lives and love, of farewell.
We linger in their whispered grace,
Strolling through ages, face to face.

With every stride a century turns,
The lessons learned, the bridges burned.
Yet forward still our journey weaves,
Through pages of forgotten leaves.

The world evolves, yet we remain,
Connected by an unseen chain.
In histories, our paths entwine,
Strolling through the sands of time.

And though we move, forever paced,
The past with present interlaced.
As ancient echoes lead our way,
We stroll through ages, night and day.

# A Measured Pace

With steady hearts we set our course,
No need for haste, no urge for force.
In measured pace, we find our stride,
With every step, we're unified.

The world around a living tale,
We walk through valleys, cross the vale.
In humble quiet, no race we trace,
As life unfolds, at a measured pace.

Together bound, with eyes so bright,
We march through shadows, into light.
With every breath, we claim our space,
In perfect calm, at our own pace.

The path we tread both old and new,
With every step a clearer view.
No faster need, no slower grace,
Just us and time, a measured pace.

In synch with life, our hearts aligned,
Each beat a step, our pace defined.
No rush to end, no dream to chase,
Together found, in measured pace.

# Deliberate Paths

On deliberate paths we tread,
Each step measured, each word said,
No rush binds our careful pace,
As we move with timeless grace.

Choices carved from thoughts refined,
Intentions pure, intentions kind,
Through forests dense and valleys wide,
We find our way, our trusted guide.

With purpose clear and destiny,
Our hearts align in harmony,
Silence speaks in whispers soft,
Guiding us through landscapes oft.

The journey's end, a distant shore,
Promises of something more,
In every step, a tale profound,
On deliberate paths, we're bound.

So let's embrace this steady climb,
Where patience turns the wheels of time,
For in each stride, we truly find,
The essence of our thoughtful mind.

## Subtle Sauntering

With subtle steps in morning's light,
We saunter through the fields so bright,
Where dew-kissed petals touch the sky,
And gentle breezes softly sigh.

Our whispers blend with nature's song,
In harmony, we move along,
No haste, no rush, just calm and peace,
As moments stretch and worries cease.

Each breath a testament to joy,
Each heartbeat like a sunlit buoy,
In rhythm with the earth's own grace,
We saunter, finding our own space.

Through meadows green and rivers bright,
Our spirits lifted weightless, light,
With every step, we stories weave,
In subtle sauntering, we believe.

So here we walk, in slow embrace,
Through time and space, no need to race,
In every glance, a promise pure,
In subtle sauntering, we endure.

# Ethereal Excursions

In ethereal excursions, we take flight,
Through azure days and starry night,
Where dreams are woven, silken thread,
In realms where only hearts have tread.

Above the clouds and past the sun,
Our souls in sync, forever run,
With whispered wings and tender gaze,
We float through endless, timeless maze.

The cosmos bends to our embrace,
In this transcendent, boundless space,
Where time dissolves and shadows play,
On ethereal excursions, we stay.

Each constellation marks our path,
Through cosmic winds, celestial bath,
In symphonies of light we dance,
With every glance, a sacred chance.

So let us drift on zephyrs' breath,
Beyond the realms of life and death,
In ethereal excursions find,
The boundless beauty of the mind.

## Leisurely Passages

In leisurely passages, time unfolds,
A tapestry of tales untold,
With measured pace and heart at ease,
We wander through life's gentle pleas.

No hurried steps, no frantic race,
Just peaceful moments we embrace,
Through pathways lined with autumn gold,
We savor stories yet to be told.

Our laughter echoes through the glen,
Where ancient trees and flowers blend,
In every step, a song we hear,
A melody both rich and clear.

Through sunlit lanes and shadowed nooks,
We turn the pages of our books,
In leisurely passages, we find,
The wonders of a tranquil mind.

So let us walk this graceful trail,
With every breath, our hearts regale,
In every moment, pure and true,
In leisurely passages, anew.

# Patient Perambulations

Wandering through the morning mists,
With steady steps and quiet twists,
I find a path that softly blends,
In nature's arms where stillness mends.

The trees they whisper tales of yore,
In time's embrace, they offer more,
A canopy of thoughts unwind,
Serenity in peace I find.

Pebbles underfoot they tell,
A journey's song, a silent spell,
In patient gait, I stroll anew,
Each stride a timeless rendezvous.

Breezes gentle, kiss the cheek,
In patient perambulations, seek,
A rhythm slow yet deeply kind,
A dance of soul and heart aligned.

## Lingering Lines

In letters left from days gone by,
I trace the words, I touch the sky,
Each line a bridge from heart to heart,
A tender craft, an olden art.

The ink it whispers, never fades,
In shadows cast by sunset's shades,
A language rich with love's refrain,
Where memories are softly lain.

From page to page I drift along,
A siren's call, a siren's song,
Each letter curves in graceful dance,
A timeless, endless, sweet romance.

With every line, a moment stirs,
A fleeting touch on life that purrs,
Lingering like the twilight hues,
In these lines, my soul renews.

# Graceful Gallivanting

Through meadows lush where daisies sway,
In light of dawn or twilight gray,
I wander wide with heart so free,
In graceful gallivanting spree.

The brook it babbles secrets sweet,
A melody beneath my feet,
I dance along the winding shores,
In nature's arms forevermore.

With every turn, a new delight,
The world unfolds in softest light,
And laughter rings from hill to glen,
A joyous echo once again.

In whispered winds and rustling leaves,
A tale of wonder each day weaves,
In graceful gallivanting stride,
Life's wonders beckon, none can hide.

## Echoes in Ease

Within the calm of evening's glow,
Where whispers of the past bestow,
An echo soft, a gentle breeze,
In quiet moments, hearts find ease.

The twilight hums a lullaby,
Beneath the canopy of sky,
Stars awaken one by one,
In silent splendor, night's begun.

Waves that lap on distant shores,
Carry tales of ancient lores,
In every ripple, every sigh,
A comfort found as time goes by.

With every echo, every tone,
A sense of peace, a world well known,
In ease we find the whispers' flow,
The tender heart of night aglow.

## Velvet Voyages

In whispers of the night, we sail,
Velvet dreams beneath the pale,
Softly across the moonlit veil,
To where the stars unveil their tale.

Through silver seas and ebony skies,
We drift on winds of lullabies,
Whispers echo sweet goodbyes,
In velvet voyages, our spirits rise.

Glimmering isles of endless sleep,
Promises made in oceans deep,
Secrets that the shadows keep,
Through velvet voyages, we softly creep.

As twilight fades to morning bright,
We anchor in the dawn's first light,
Our souls alight with endless might,
From velvet voyages of the night.

Hearts aglow in dreams untold,
In velvet hues of soft and bold,
Endless stories yet unfold,
On velvet voyages, pure and old.

# Ease Through Eternity

In realms where time moves slow,
Eternity's calm rivers flow,
Soft breezes in the starlight glow,
To endless dreams, our hearts bestow.

Life's chaos fades to gentle ease,
In tranquil waves upon the seas,
Moments lingering like trees,
Eternal whispers in the breeze.

Through meadows of the mind, we find,
A place where time and soul entwined,
Easing through the vast and kind,
Eternity in peace designed.

Stars above in silence gleam,
Guiding us through timeless seam,
A river of enduring dream,
In eternity's soft glowing beam.

With hearts that ebb and spirits soar,
Through eternity, we implore,
A tranquil journey evermore,
Ease through time's infinite door.

# Hushed Journeys

In shadows deep where whispers lie,
We tread the paths where dreams fly,
Underneath a muted sky,
On hushed journeys, you and I.

Silent echoes lead the way,
Through nights transformed to silver day,
Whispers in the twilight play,
On hushed journeys, come what may.

Steps are light like morning dew,
Unseen paths that we pursue,
In mysteries old yet ever new,
Hushed journeys bind us, true.

Along soft trails, our spirits blend,
To places where the shadows bend,
On hushed journeys without end,
Silent, endless, we descend.

Twilight's secrets in the air,
Guiding us with gentle care,
Hushed journeys take us where,
Dreams and memories both share.

## Reticent Rambles

Through forests dense where shadows play,
We walk in silence, light of day,
Whispered words along the way,
In reticent rambles, we will stay.

On paths that twist in quiet thoughts,
Reticent rambles, no words caught,
Silent woods with secrets fraught,
In silent journeys, souls are sought.

With sun above in muted grace,
We find our steps in this still place,
Reticent rambles set the pace,
In nature's arms, a soft embrace.

Birdsongs weave through the tranquil air,
Guiding us with tender care,
In reticent rambles, void of glare,
We leave behind our worldly wear.

Our hearts attune to nature's sound,
In every leaf and mossy ground,
Reticent rambles, profound,
In silent journeys, peace is found.

# Poised Promenades

Beneath the whispering canopy,
Shadows stretch and gently lean,
Footsteps echo soft and slow,
A tranquil walk through emerald sheen.

Marigolds line the winding path,
Their golden faces greet the dawn,
Deftly we stroll amid the hue,
Where earth and sky adorn.

In poised promenades we intertwine,
Hearts aligned with nature's breath,
Each step a dance of silent grace,
In harmony devoid of death.

Birds compose their melodies,
While leaves applaud with rustling sound,
A symphony of serene delight,
In each promenade found.

Time drifts on in soft repose,
On paths where dreams and notions flow,
In these poised promenades so dear,
Together, we let go.

## Minute by Minute

Seconds drip like morning dew,
To nourish roots of future days,
Minute by minute life sustains,
Unfolding in mysterious ways.

Silent whispers of each tick,
Resonate through hearts and minds,
Minute by minute shadows fade,
Revealing moments intertwined.

Golden rays from azure skies,
Cast their warmth on time's expanse,
Minute by minute night retreats,
Daylight claims its tender chance.

Thoughts cascade like fountains free,
In the river of our hearts,
Minute by minute currents guide,
To where our dreams depart.

Unseen forces shape our fate,
In the symphony of time,
Minute by minute stars align,
Crafting moments so sublime.

# Subdued Steps

Muffled footfalls on the path,
As twilight cloaks the world in grey,
Subdued steps in evening's grace,
Guide us till the break of day.

Whispers ride the cooling breeze,
Through trees that guard our gentle stroll,
Subdued steps in silence tread,
Where shadows find their soul.

Each step a testament of peace,
In the realm where echoes hush,
Subdued steps in harmony,
Dissolving in the twilight's blush.

Stars above begin to gleam,
Their light a tape of dreams unfurled,
Subdued steps with subtle gleam,
We roam this softened world.

Time suspends its hurried march,
In the cadence of our pace,
Subdued steps, a quiet dance,
Through night's tender embrace.

## Ponderous Paces

Wandering through fields of thought,
Where every step could change our fate,
Ponderous paces carry us,
To moments where we contemplate.

Furrowed brows and pensive hearts,
Reflect the journey deep inside,
Ponderous paces mark the way,
Through valleys vast and wide.

Each footfall is a question posed,
Seeking truths beneath the veil,
Ponderous paces take their time,
Where musings never fail.

Underneath the starry dome,
We find our thoughts both light and grand,
Ponderous paces set the tone,
As we navigate this land.

Pondering life's winding route,
In pace both somber and profound,
Each step an echo in the soul,
With wisdom gently crowned.

# Languid Steps

In twilight's hush, the earth holds still,
Soft whispers through the evening chill,
Languid steps on paths unknown,
Where daylight fades, and dreams are sewn.

The stars awaken, one by one,
A tapestry the night has spun,
Each step I take, a breathy wisp,
Of moonlit trails in silent crisp.

Leaves underfoot, a velvet tread,
Where stories of the night are spread,
In every pause, a secret keeps,
A world that wakes as daylight sleeps.

Shadows dance upon the stones,
Mysteries in lowered tones,
Languid steps, a gentle glide,
Through night's embrace, the soul's own guide.

In starlight's glow, the paths unfold,
Languid steps through dreams untold,
A journey through the night's expanse,
In languid steps, a twilight dance.

## Gradual Glimpses

Beneath the dawn, the world renews,
With gradual glimpses of soft hues,
Each morning brings its gentle light,
A canvas kissed by silent night.

The skies are brushed with tender care,
Soft whispers float upon the air,
Gradual glimpses of the day,
In shadows that now fade away.

The morning dew on petals cling,
Awakening as robins sing,
Each glance unveils a hidden grace,
In every sunbeam's warm embrace.

Through sleepy mists, the world does rise,
Revealing wonders to the eyes,
Gradual glimpses lead the way,
To treasures in the light of day.

With each soft turn, and each new gaze,
Gradual glimpses fill the days,
A world reborn with gentle light,
In glimpses of the morning bright.

# Serene Strolls

Between the hills where rivers flow,
Serene strolls through meadows go,
With every step, a peaceful sigh,
Beneath the vast and tranquil sky.

The breeze it whispers, gentle, sweet,
As grass sways lightly at my feet,
Serene strolls in nature's glee,
Where silence sings a melody.

Along the path, the flowers bloom,
Their fragrance fills the air with plume,
In serene strolls, my heart takes flight,
Through fields ablaze with summer's light.

The sun, it dances on the lake,
Where mirrored dreams in ripples break,
Serene strolls by water's edge,
A vow beneath the willow's pledge.

With every breath, the world seems whole,
In serene strolls, it heals the soul,
A journey through the calm and clear,
Where peace is found in moments dear.

## Steps of Solitude

In quiet lanes where shadows bend,
The steps of solitude descend,
Each footfall is a whispered tone,
Of time that's spent in thought alone.

The world retreats, a hushed embrace,
In solitude, there's boundless space,
Steps of solitude, calm and wide,
Where inner worlds and thoughts abide.

The twilight hour, a soft caress,
Secrets shared in quietness,
Steps of solitude, gentle trace,
Of moments wrapped in silent grace.

Through forest paths and silent fields,
A sanctuary the silence yields,
Steps of solitude, tender strides,
Where soul and self in peace resides.

The moon above, a watchful eye,
Lights the path where heartbeats lie,
Steps of solitude, pure and true,
A walk where dreams and stillness grew.

# Echoes of Soft Footsteps

Beneath the whispered trees, we tread,
In twilight's tender, fleeting smile,
The moon above, our path it led,
We walked together, mile by mile.

Soft echoes in the dusk's embrace,
The world seemed still, with bated breath,
Each step we took, a gentle trace,
Of love that outlasts life and death.

Footfalls wrapped in quiet grace,
As stars adorned the evening's shawl,
Our shadows danced in silent place,
A tender waltz, a secret call.

Beneath the canopy of night,
Life's hurried pace began to slow,
In every step, a pure delight,
As moonlight set our hearts aglow.

In memories these paths remain,
Where night's soft echoes softly seep,
A dance of footsteps in the rain,
Until the world falls into sleep.

## Strolls in the Afterglow

The sunset bathes the world in gold,
As day gives way to evening's sigh,
Hand in hand, we silently stroll,
Underneath the painted sky.

The afterglow, a fleeting art,
Brushstrokes of warmth across the land,
We walk with twilight in our hearts,
Our shadows stretching hand in hand.

Whispered secrets, soft and low,
Beneath the sky's kaleidoscope,
With every step, like rivers flow,
Into the sea of dreams and hope.

The world awaits the stars' reveal,
As night's first breaths begin to show,
In silence, words we do not feel,
But stroll along in afterglow.

In this twilight, moments freeze,
Preserved in time's ephemeral light,
The afterglow in memories,
A gentle kiss from fading night.

# Rhythms of Reflection

Upon the stillness of the lake,
Their rippled glass, the stars reflect,
In quiet nights, a heart will ache,
For truths that we cannot neglect.

The rhythms of reflection sing,
In patterns danced by evening's breath,
A song of every living thing,
Of life and loss, of love and death.

Each ripple tells a tale anew,
Of laughter, tears, of joy, despair,
A mirror to the hearts we knew,
In moonlit calm, away from care.

By water's edge, in silent night,
We find ourselves within its face,
Reflections of a hidden light,
A journey in this tranquil space.

In rhythms of the water's sweep,
We see what words cannot convey,
The secrets that in silence keep,
And guide our hearts upon their way.

## Meandering Through Moments

We wander paths of time and thought,
Where moments blend in streams of life,
Through memories by fate inwrought,
Both bitter-sweet and rife with strife.

Each step we take through past's embrace,
A silent echo of what's been,
In winding trails, we find a trace,
Of dreams once lost and found again.

Breathing in this gentle flow,
We dance along a temporal seam,
Moments come, as moments go,
In waking hours, and in dream.

Meandering through days gone by,
We stitch our story, thread by thread,
In laughter, tears, our souls defy,
The fleeting tears that we shed.

As moments weave into a whole,
A tapestry of life unfurled,
They guide the pathways of the soul,
Through visions of a timeless world.

# Unhurried Journeys

Along the path of morning dew,
Where sunlight paints a golden hue,
With every step so gentle and light,
Embrace the calm of day and night.

The world unfolds at measured pace,
No rush to win this quiet race,
In stillness find the heart's delight,
And let the moments take their flight.

Through meadows rich with fragrant bloom,
And whispering woods where shadows loom,
Discover wonders, near and far,
Beneath the endless, watching star.

Every breath a gift so rare,
Each heartbeat tells a tale to share,
Time a tapestry we weave,
In unhurried journeys, we believe.

So walk this life with patient stride,
Let intuition be your guide,
For treasures wait in every turn,
And simple joys in hearts will burn.

# The Art of Strolling

With every step and measured beat,
Feel the earth beneath your feet,
In leisurely and thoughtful stroll,
Find the whispers of your soul.

Past the streams and shaded nooks,
Where nature's voice is all it took,
To guide you through the hidden lanes,
Where peace resides and quiet reigns.

In the hustle, find your space,
Savoring moments, setting pace,
A stroll is more than mere delay,
A mindful journey through the day.

Pause to watch the leaves that fall,
and hear the distant bird's sweet call,
In stillness, find your heart's own beat,
And make each strolling hour complete.

Through winding paths where dreams unfold,
In every step, a story told,
The art of strolling—blissful, free,
Unlocking life's soft mystery.

## Winding with Care

Down dim-lit paths where silence weaves,
A journey where the heart believes,
In winding trails with care explored,
Life's gentle whispers are adored.

With every step, a careful choice,
To listen to the inner voice,
That leads through shadows, light and shade,
In trust of paths a heart has made.

Through valleys lush and hills that soar,
Discover what you've longed for,
In curvature of earth and time,
Find beauty in the quiet rhyme.

Glistening streams narrate the tale,
Of journeys slow and spirits hale,
In winding ways where dreams take flight,
And cultivate the deep insight.

So walk with care and mindful gaze,
In labyrinths where sunlight plays,
For winding paths hold precious lore,
And open up the heart's own door.

## Peaceful Wanderings

Beneath the sky that sways so blue,
In emerald fields with morning dew,
Walk softly through the dawning light,
Embrace the calm and purest sight.

In forests deep where echoes dream,
And by the gently flowing stream,
Find solace in the rustling leaves,
And every breath that nature breathes.

With every step let worries cease,
In wanderings that whisper peace,
Amidst the blooms and open skies,
Let quiet thoughts within you rise.

Through sandy shores and desert air,
Where time dissolves without a care,
Each footstep finds a sacred ground,
In wandering peace where hearts are found.

So journey forth with tranquil mind,
In peaceful wanderings, treasures find,
For in the stillness, beauty grows,
And life's serene and gentle flows.

# Unhurried Ventures

Through valleys green and skies so vast,
We wander slow, no need to rush.
Each tree and leaf a time to cast,
In whispered winds, our souls we hush.

No clock to bind us, paths unfurl,
With every step, a story spun.
Embracing moments in this world,
While shadows dance beneath the sun.

Soft melodies of rivers' flow,
Serenade our hearts with grace.
The world less frantic, moving slow,
In nature's arms, a warm embrace.

Mountains greet us with a nod,
Their peaks, a testament of time.
Silent witnesses of each trod,
Our spirits lifted in their climb.

Unhurried ventures through the land,
With patience as our guiding star.
Together, hand in gentle hand,
We find ourselves in realms afar.

## Gentle Glide

On silver streams our vessels drift,
The world a blur in twilight's hue.
Each ripple sends a tender gift,
Of dreams and thoughts both old and new.

Soft whispers from the willow trees,
Their branches trailing in the tide.
With every breath, a care it frees,
As on we sail, in gentle glide.

No captain here but dawn's first light,
No compass but the stars above.
In every gaze a pure delight,
As nature sings her song of love.

We find in silence sweet reprieve,
From all life's hurried, frantic pace.
In every wave, a chance to weave,
Our hopes and joy with soft embrace.

Onward through the realms of peace,
With hearts unburdened, souls aligned.
The gentle glide will never cease,
In waters calm, our paths defined.

## Mellow Marches

Across the fields where daisies grow,
We march in time with heart's own beat.
In mellow steps, through ebb and flow,
Life's quiet rhythms we do greet.

The skies above, a canvas bright,
With hues that blend in morning's rise.
We walk with care, in softest light,
A peaceful journey, no disguise.

Through arching trees and whispers low,
Our breaths in sync with nature's pace.
Each forward step in vibrant glow,
A gentle march through time and space.

No rush to be where we must end,
The journey holds its own reward.
In every stride, we find a friend,
In every scene, a chord adored.

Mellow marches, slow and dear,
Through life's vast fields forever wide.
With every footfall, banish fear,
In steps of grace, side by side.

## Ambling Ascensions

Over hills and through the glen,
We climb with steady, patient gait.
The path unwinds beyond our ken,
To distant heights, we walk, elate.

Each step an echo, soft and clear,
In valleys deep and peaks above.
With hearts unburdened, minds sincere,
We tread the paths of endless love.

The air grows thin but spirit high,
As vistas open wide below.
In slow ascent, we touch the sky,
In ambling pace, our hearts a-glow.

No summit rush, the journey's key,
In every stride a truth revealed.
The mountain knows our souls set free,
In steps so slow yet unconcealed.

Ambling ascensions, bold yet meek,
With every footfall, purpose found.
In life's grand climb, the summit seek,
Through patient steps on sacred ground.

Milton Keynes UK
Ingram Content Group UK Ltd.
UKHW050131130724
445613UK00003B/42